T0011803

Life Cycle of a Turtle

by Meg Gaertner

FOCUS READERS

PIONEER

www.focusreaders.com

Focus Readers is distributed by North Star Editions: sales@northstareditions.com | 888-417-0195

Produced for Focus Readers by Red Line Editorial.

Photographs ©: iStockphoto, cover, 1, 4, 9, 10, 13, 14, 17; Shutterstock Images, 7, 18, 21

Library of Congress Cataloging-in-Publication Data
Names: Gaertner, Meg, author.
Title: Life cycle of a turtle / by Meg Gaertner.
Description: Lake Elmo, MN : Focus Readers, [2022] | Series: Life
   cycles | Includes index. | Audience: Grades 2-3
Identifiers: LCCN 2021007326 (print) | LCCN 2021007327 (ebook) | ISBN
   9781644938331 (hardcover) | ISBN 9781644938799 (paperback) | ISBN
   9781644939253 (ebook) | ISBN 9781644939697 (pdf)
Subjects: LCSH: Turtles--Life cycles--Juvenile literature.
Classification: LCC QL666.C5 G337 2022 (print) | LCC QL666.C5 (ebook) |
   DDC 597.92156--dc23
LC record available at https://lccn.loc.gov/2021007326
LC ebook record available at https://lccn.loc.gov/2021007327

Printed in the United States of America
Mankato, MN
082021

About the Author

Meg Gaertner enjoys reading, writing, dancing, and being outside. She lives in Minnesota.

Table of Contents

Chapter 1

Egg

A **male** turtle and **female** turtle come together. They **mate**. Then the female turtle finds a good place to dig. She might go to a beach. Or she might go to the side of a river.

The female turtle digs a hole. She uses her back legs. She lays eggs in the hole. She covers them with loose soil or sand. Then she leaves.

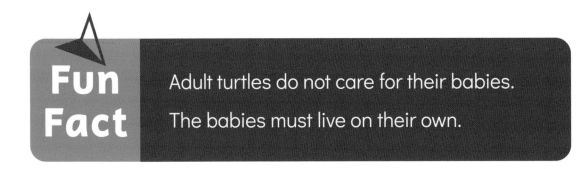

Fun Fact

Adult turtles do not care for their babies. The babies must live on their own.

back leg

Embryo

An **embryo** grows inside each egg. Embryos grow faster in warmer weather. They grow slower when it is cooler. The weather also affects if the embryos will be male or female. Cooler weather results in more male embryos. Eventually, the eggs are ready to **hatch**.

Chapter 2

Hatchling

Hatchlings have little bumps on their noses. They use the bumps to poke holes in the eggshells. The holes get bigger.

The hatchlings come out of the eggs. They dig up through the soil or sand. They dig out of the nest. They reach the open air.

Fun Fact

Sea turtle hatchlings leave their nests at night. That way, they are in less danger from other animals.

Chapter 3

Young Turtle

Some hatchlings move to water. This could be the ocean or a pond. Other hatchlings hide near plants. They all try to stay safe from other animals.

Young turtles grow over time. Some eat fish and frogs. Others eat insects and snails. And others eat plants. It depends on the type of turtle.

Fun Fact

Turtles do not have teeth. But their mouths have sharp edges. They use these edges to cut food.

Chapter 4

Adult Turtle

Young turtles grow into **mature** adults. Many turtles have hard shells. They **bask** in the sun. Most turtles also spend time in water.

Adult turtles mate when the weather warms. Female turtles dig nests. Female sea turtles even return to the beaches where they hatched. They travel great distances to do so.

Female turtles lay their eggs in the nests. The life cycle continues.

Life Cycle Stages

Egg

Hatchling

Young Turtle

Adult
Turtle

FOCUS ON
Turtle Life Cycles

Write your answers on a separate piece of paper.

1. Write a sentence describing how weather affects a turtle embryo's growth.

2. Which stage of the life cycle do you find most interesting? Why?

3. What do turtles have instead of teeth?
   - A. tiny bumps on their noses
   - B. sharp edges on their mouths
   - C. hard shells on their bodies

4. Why does a female turtle cover her eggs with soil or sand?
   - A. so she can find the eggs again later
   - B. to keep the eggs cool so they grow faster
   - C. to keep the eggs safe and out of sight

Answer key on page 24.

Glossary

bask
To lie in sunlight for warmth.

embryo
A stage of growth that happens before birth or hatching.

female
Able to have babies or lay eggs.

hatch
To break open so a young animal can come out.

hatchlings
Young animals that just came out of their eggs.

male
Unable to have babies or lay eggs.

mate
To come together to make a baby.

mature
Fully grown.

To Learn More

BOOKS

Hansen, Grace. *Leatherback Turtle Migration*. Minneapolis: Abdo Publishing, 2018.

Owings, Lisa. *From Egg to Sea Turtle*. Minneapolis: Lerner Publications, 2017.

NOTE TO EDUCATORS

Visit **www.focusreaders.com** to find lesson plans, activities, links, and other resources related to this title.

Index

Answer Key: **1.** Answers will vary; **2.** Answers will vary; **3.** B; **4.** C